REST IN

&

A Calamity in Contemporary Christianity

Iain H. Murray

THE BANNER OF TRUTH TRUST

THE BANNER OF TRUTH TRUST

3 Murrayfield Road, Edinburgh EH12 6EL, UK
PO Box 621, Carlisle, PA 17013, USA

∽

© The Banner of Truth Trust 2010

ISBN: 978 1 84871 081 8

∽

Typeset in 11/14 pt Adobe Garamond Pro at
The Banner of Truth Trust
Printed in the USA by
VersaPress, Inc.,
East Peoria, IL

Unless otherwise stated all Scripture quotation are from
the New American Standard Bible © Lockman Foundation 1977

CONTENTS

Then God blessed the seventh day and sanctified it, because in it
He rested from all His work which God had created and made.
GENESIS 2:3

What is believed about God is the most important thing in life. And it is because man's greatest need is for the true knowledge of God that the Bible stands alone. It is the only revelation of God in words that he has himself given. To open its pages is to be surrounded by truth about his being and nature. Here are statements on which faith may be surely grounded, and among these statements the text above is one of the most fundamental. It introduces us to two words which run through Scripture, the words 'sanctify' and 'rest'.[1]

Both of these words speak to us of God. The first, to 'sanctify' means to 'make holy', 'to separate', or to 'set apart'. God himself is holy; uniquely that is his title. What he sanctifies is something which belongs to him, and the verse therefore indicates that in a special way the seventh day belongs to him. 'God blessed the seventh day and sanctified it'.

---

[1] I am not here concerned to defend the historicity of the Genesis account of creation. According to Scripture, understanding creation begins with faith (*Heb.* 11:3), which faith is itself born of the same creating power by which the believer has been brought from death to life (*2 Cor.* 4:6). Christ attributes the words of Genesis chapter 2 to the Creator (*Matt.*19:4-5). 'The one who believes in the Son of God has the witness [testimony] in himself' (*1 John* 5:10).

The second word, also introduced immediately after the creation, is 'rest', God 'rested'. In the original, he *sabbatised,* from which came the word 'sabbath' (or 'rest'). The statement may appear a contradiction. How can an omnipotent Creator of the universe be said to 'rest'? Elsewhere in Scripture it is expressly denied that the Everlasting God can be 'weary or tired'(*Isa.* 40:28), and Christ denied that God ceased to work on the seventh day (*John* 5:17).

The explanation lies in a right understanding of the word 'rest'. It does not mean inactivity. It has to do rather with God's reflection on his completed creation. Six times in Genesis 1:4-25, we are told that all God made was 'good', and that chapter concludes, 'And God saw all that He had made, and behold, it was very good' (1:31). All was 'good' because all fulfilled the purpose for which he had created, namely, the display of his own glory. 'The heavens are telling of the glory of God' (*Psa.* 19:1). The world is the temple of God, 'And in His temple everything says, "Glory"' (*Psa.* 29:9). The splendour of creation — from flowers and birds, to oceans and furthest galaxies — declares to man that God is great and wise and good. All things come from God, and he is to be adored for all.

'God rested' means that as he surveyed his work he was satisfied. He took pleasure in it, and that because he delights in his own glory. In other words, God's rest is in himself.[2] Augustine

---

[2] On the words the Lord 'rested and was refreshed' (*Exod.* 31:17, AV), Geerhardus Vos noted: '"Rest" has in Scripture, in fact to the Shemitic mind generally, a positive rather than a negative import. It stands for consummation of a work accomplished and the joy and satisfaction attendant upon this.' (*Biblical Theology,* Edinburgh, Banner of Truth, 1974), p. 140. 'He took great complacency in what he had done, as that which was suited to the end aimed at, namely, the expression of his greatness, goodness, and wisdom, unto his rational creatures' (John Owen, 'Exercitations Concerning the Name, Original, Nature, Use, and Continuance of a Day of Sacred Rest', *Exposition of Hebrews* (repr. Edinburgh:

saw the meaning long ago when he prayed: 'After all thy works of creation which were very good, thou didst rest on the seventh day, although thou hadst created them all in unbroken rest . . . thou art the Good, and needest no rest, and art always at rest, because thou thyself art thy own rest.'[3]

IS GENESIS 2:3 FOR US?

But for what purpose is this statement about God sanctifying the seventh day and resting made known to us? That question takes us to the reason why many pass lightly over the words of Genesis 2:3. An answer commonly given is that while the words speak about God, they include no mandate or direction for man to follow, no model for human behaviour. Therefore, it is said, any idea that a seventh part of man's time belongs in a special way to God is not taught in Genesis 2:3; it belongs rather to a much later date in Scripture in the time of Moses.

A great deal depends on whether this understanding of the verse is right or wrong. I offer these reasons for believing it is wrong:

1. The words 'God blessed the seventh day' are not the first notice of blessing in this narrative. There was blessing on the creation (*Gen.* 1:22), and blessing on man — 'male and female He created them. And God blessed them; and God said to them, "Be fruitful and multiply, and fill the earth, and subdue it"' (*Gen.*

Banner of Truth, 1991), vol. 2, p. 334).
[3] Augustine, *Confessions and Enchiridion,* Library of Christian Classics, ed. Albert C. Outler (London: SCM, 1955), p. 332.

1:27-8). That God blessed a day for his own, and not for man's good, would be a usage of the word out of harmony not only with this passage but with the whole of Scripture.

2. It was clearly revealed to man at the beginning why he was created: 'God created man in His own image, in the image of God He created him; male and female He created them' (*Gen.* 1:27). Man was not made for himself. He exists for God and for fellowship with him. He was therefore made in the likeness of God. He is to love and delight in what God delights, that is in God himself. That is the purpose of his existence (*Matt.* 22:37). It is unthinkable that this was true at the creation, and yet not known to man himself. To be holy as God is holy (*Lev.* 20:26; *1 Pet.* 1:16) was a truth implanted in man's very being, and therein lay his obligation to obedience. It is surely in the context of man's recognition of himself, as made in the image of God, with his life to be patterned on that of his Creator, that the words of Genesis 2:3 are to be understood. There is a day God sanctified for man: as God rests in himself so man is to rest in God. *Therein lies true happiness and satisfaction.* By so marking the day, man was to enter into its blessing; glorifying God and enjoying him belong together. To quote Augustine again: 'Thou hast made us for thyself, and our hearts are restless until they find their rest in thee.'[4]

If this is the right understanding of Genesis 2:3 — and it is difficult to know any other — then we may conclude that the example of God stated in that verse was provided for man's imitation and instruction.[5]

---

[4] For a fuller treatment of what this means, see John Piper, *The Pleasures of God: Meditations on God's Delight in Being God* (Sisters, OR:Multnomah, 2000).
[5] That God 'sanctified' one day in seven for unfallen man is enough for us to

3. The division of time into a seven-day week is best understood as originating at the creation and in connexion with Genesis 2:3. Those who believe that a day of rest did not come into being until the law was given through Moses at Sinai have no explanation how a seven-day time cycle came to pre-date that event. But they reply, if a 'rest day' (Sabbath) came down from creation there would be references to it before Sinai. It is true there is an absence of such references, yet that is not altogether surprising. Man, after the Fall, instead of finding satisfaction in God, preferred the creature to the Creator. In the words of Jeremiah, 'They have forsaken Me, The fountain of living waters' (*Jer.* 2:13). Even so, traces of the rest originally appointed by God were not wholly obliterated. The passage of time in terms of seven days is noted in Genesis 8:10, 12, and in the life of Jacob we find Laban referring to the duration of a week (*Gen.* 29:27-8).[6] But where did such a division of time come from? Man could not deduce a seven-day week either from a solar year or from a lunar month. The best explanation for the week goes back to Genesis 2.

---

know, without asking why it could be so if all man's days were to be lived for the glory of God. But the question is also relevant for the Christian. Abraham Kuyper gives this line of answer: 'Six days we have to spend in the fulfilment of our earthly duties, and one of the seven we have to consecrate to the more special service of the Lord. Of course, we should serve the Lord all the seven days. The difference between the two can never be other than a partial one. During the six days appointed to labour, all that concerns our outward life is prominent. On the Lord's day, on the contrary, it is the special service of the Lord that should dominate us . . . during the weekdays it is to a great extent a mediate serving the Lord, during and in our work, and that on the day of rest there should be an almost exclusive serving of our God in the immediate form of adoration and of drinking out of the Fountain of Life.' 'The Lord's Day Observance', Address by Abraham Kuyper in *Sunday The World's Rest Day* (New York; NY Sabbath Committee, 1916), pp. 56-7. Apart from a few chapters this is a poor volume.

[6] 'Week' is not a Hebrew term as such, but the Hebrew word speaks of a period of seven days.

There is, however, stronger evidence that some knowledge of what God had earlier appointed survived. In Exodus chapter 16 there is a narrative of experiences that would otherwise be incomprehensible. Between the time of creation and the exodus from Egypt, thousands of years had passed. How unworthy the children of Israel were of their deliverance from Egypt is demonstrated by their behaviour in the wilderness. They complained that instead of being blessed by God they were likely to die of hunger, and God answered their unbelief by the miracle of which we read in Exodus 16:4-5: 'Then the Lord said to Moses, "Behold, I will rain bread from heaven for you; and the people shall go out and gather a day's portion every day . . . And it will come about on the sixth day, when they prepare what they bring in, it will be twice as much as they gather daily."'

'The sixth day' points to an existing knowledge of time divided by weeks. Still more significant, the text just quoted gives no explanation why, on the sixth day, twice the amount of manna would be given from heaven. The people were told that if manna was kept overnight on any of five days it would become foul. But on the sixth day, when twice the amount was given, half was to be deliberately kept for eating on the following day. Accordingly we read of the sixth day: 'So they put it aside until morning, as Moses had ordered, and it did not become foul, nor was there any worm in it. And Moses said, "Eat it today, for today is a sabbath to the Lord; today you will not find it in the field. Six days you shall gather it, but on the seventh day, the sabbath, there will be none."' (*Exod.* 16:24-26). Some, not believing the word of God, and wanting manna every day, ignored the command of God and went out to collect it: 'but they found none' (16:27).

God specifically stated the purpose of this miracle, 'that I may test them, whether they will walk in my law or not' (16:4, NKJV).

How could this be a test unless direction regarding the seventh day had not been already given? Nothing in Exodus 16 suggests that the appointment of a special seventh day of rest was only now being introduced. Had the manna miracle of Exodus 16 followed the giving of the ten commandments in Exodus 20, we would have understood the fourth commandment as the foundation for the 'test'. But that was plainly a later event at Sinai. Further, when we come to the wording of that fourth commandment, its language confirms that the Sabbath was not new but already existing. The commandment does not begin, 'Know there is a Sabbath day', but '*Remember* . . .'; and what is to be remembered is specifically identified with Genesis 2:3:

> Remember the sabbath day, to keep it holy. Six days you shall labor and do all your work, but the seventh day is a sabbath of the Lord your God; in it you shall not do any work, you or your son or your daughter . . . For in six days the Lord made the heavens and the earth, the sea and all that is in them, and rested on the seventh day; therefore the Lord blessed the sabbath day and made it holy (*Exod.* 20:8-11).

To meet the force of the last paragraph, another explanation of the words it contains from Genesis 2 has been offered. It is that the words of Genesis 2:3 do not assert the establishment of the seventh day pattern at the time of the creation, but Moses inserted them at that point in Genesis because of what God meant to appoint for Israel at this much later date. So the quotation from Genesis 2:3 (in *Exod.* 20:11) was to give authority to a commandment intended only for the Jews, not for mankind. This interpretation surely requires a contorted reading of Genesis 2:3. It is the same as saying that God did not 'bless' any day at that time; rather, he delayed the blessing until a few thousand years later.[7] In the comment of Charles Hodge: 'It is an unnatural interpretation which no one would adopt except to suit a purpose. The narrative [of Genesis] purports to be what God did at the time of creation.'[8] Patrick Fairbairn attributes the origin of this idea to the 'fond conceit of some Jewish Rabbins, who sought thereby to magnify their nation, and was adopted only by such Christian divines as had already made up their minds on the temporary obligation of the Sabbath.'[9]

This is no discussion of minor significance. As I have said, a great deal depends on which conclusion is right and which wrong. If the appointment of the day of rest comes from the time of creation, then the words of the Lord, 'The Sabbath was made for man' (*Mark* 2:27) refer to all mankind, and the fourth commandment has divine authority today. If the appointment belongs to the time of Israel, then it has no universal significance, and the fourth commandment is only for Jews.

---

[7] David Green, in an occasional paper, has commented: 'Sabbath is the final blessing of three in the creation narrative (*Gen.* 1:22, 28; 2:3). Has anyone asserted that either of the first two blessings was delayed in their effect until God gathered Israel into a nation at Sinai? Why then should the third blessing be understood as delayed?'

[8] Charles Hodge, *Systematic Theology*, vol. 3 (London and Edinburgh: Nelson, 1874), pp. 325-6.

[9] Patrick Fairbairn, *The Typology of Scripture*, vol. 2 (Edinburgh, T.&T. Clark, 1864), p. 127. 'Not what these men say, but what they prove, is to be admitted', is John Owen's comment on the Jewish rabbis, *Hebrews*, vol. 2, p. 291.

THE SABBATH AND CEREMONIAL LAW

It is agreed on all sides that a fuller teaching on the Sabbath was given at the time of Moses, and that the nation needed to be educated or re-educated in its significance at that later period: 'You made known to them your holy Sabbath' (*Neh.* 9:14, ESV). The Sabbath was also at this time related to God's redemptive purposes. It was now a memorial not only of creation but of the nation's deliverance from Egypt (*Deut.* 5:15). The special day became a covenant sign of God's saving work in their midst (*Exod.* 31:16; *Ezek.* 20:12), and special sanctions of law were introduced for its observance by the nation. For its desecration the death penalty was appointed (*Exod.* 31:14-15). Even the lighting of fires was forbidden (*Num.* 15:32-36).

From this arises the argument that, whatever the origin of the Sabbath, it was so bound up with the nation that its permanence and its laws had to end when the Jewish economy passed away. It is said to be clear from the New Testament that ceremonial law, and law that belonged to Israel as a theocracy, terminated with the new covenant.

This argument depends on the assumption that the fourth commandment is so identified with Israel that it could no longer have any place when the Old Testament economy passed away. To the contrary it may be said:

1. If the case we have given from Genesis 2:3 is sound, then it is already clear that the fourth commandment does not belong exclusively to the Jews.

2. In the Old Testament the observation of the fourth commandment was not required for Jews only but also for

the 'sojourner [alien] who stays with you' (*Exod.* 20:10; see *Neh.*13:16-18).

3. If the keeping of the Sabbath was only of ceremonial and not permanent moral significance, why was it placed by the finger of God in the centre of the moral law? The law is presented in Scripture as a reflection of the unchanging character of God. It came directly from God: 'And God spoke all these words, saying, 'I am the Lord thy God . . .' (*Exod.* 20:1-2), and was written on tables of stone. To live for his glory, not to hate, not to commit adultery, not to lie, not to covet the possessions of another — these are abiding moral laws; and in the midst of these laws stand the words, 'Remember the Sabbath day, to keep it holy.'

Further, if the fourth commandment were only of ceremonial or temporary significance why should disobedience to it be treated in Scripture as a grave, moral offence? Generally the death penalty was not required for infringement of ceremonial law, but it was for this. There is no offence against God more seriously condemned by the prophets. Something much more than the ceremonial was involved in the commandment:

A Sabbath-breaker was among the most vile and abominable characters. The whole day was to be devoted to God and religion. When they kept the day as holy, they prospered. Calamities and judgments were inflicted on them, when as a nation they neglected God's holy Sabbath. All the prophets who were raised up, one after another, called them to observe the Sabbath, warned against any contempt of it, and placed the sanctification of the Sabbath upon the footing of equality with the moral virtues.[10]

[10] Nathan Perkins, *Twenty-Four Discourses* (Hartford: Hudson & Goodwin, 1795), p. 318.

4. A cessation from activity, and the observance of external rites, was never the essence of the fourth commandment (the idea that it was being a constant error among the Jews). A pause from the ordinary labours of life was always secondary to the primary spiritual object of the seventh day. The psalm designated 'for the Sabbath day' (*Psa.* 92), shows that the right observance of the day entails reflecting on the lovingkindness, the faithfulness, the uprightness of God. It is for delight in God. 'If because of the sabbath, you turn your foot from doing your own pleasure on My holy day, and call the sabbath a delight, the holy day of the Lord honorable, and shall honor it, desisting from your own ways, from seeking your own pleasure, and speaking your own word, then you will take delight in the Lord' (*Isa.* 58:13-14). This is in harmony with Genesis 2:3 and rest in God.

5. If the fourth commandment is to be considered redundant, and no longer part of the moral law of God, why is it that the New Testament, in repeated references to man's continued obligation to the law, makes no exception? The moral law, like its author, is 'holy, and just and good' (*Rom.* 7:12, AV). It has authority over Gentile as well as Jew (*Rom.* 2:15). Children at Ephesus were to be taught the commandments (*Eph.* 6:2). Timothy is to remember, 'the Law is good' (*1 Tim.* 1:8). The apostle John says, 'Sin is the transgression of the law' (*1 John* 3:4, AV). Nowhere is there a suggestion of any exception. On the contrary James, quoting the ten commandments, writes that he who 'stumbles in one point . . . has become guilty of all' (*James* 2:10). In other words, there is a unity to the moral law. Like as sheet of glass, if broken at one point, the whole is shattered.

CALVIN'S CORRECTION

The authority of Calvin has often been quoted to support the view that the substance of the fourth commandment cannot be separated from the ceremonial law and that its authority is therefore ended for Christians. It is true this was Calvin's belief. In his *Institutes* he rejects the teaching that while 'the ceremonial part of this commandment has been abrogated . . . the moral part remains — namely, the fixing of one day in seven.'[11] But what has not been sufficiently noticed is that this did not remain the reformer's teaching. The passages on the fourth commandment found in the final edition of the *Institutes* of 1559 were written some years before that date and never revised. When preaching on Genesis, in 1559, Calvin very clearly takes the position which he earlier rejected:

Concerning the creation of God's works, it is said that 'God rested in order to consider his works'. How can that be? He did not need to, as we have stated, but he instructs us what we are to do, as if saying, 'Behold, I want a day set aside for contemplation of my works.' Therefore, we have a God who is resting to be a mirror and pattern so that we may conform ourselves to him . . .[12] Because we are so weak and fragile and fickle, God has given us a day to help us sustain ourselves for the remainder of the week . . . help will

[11] *Institutes of the Christian Religion,* ed. J. T. McNeill, translated by F. L. Battles (Philadelphia: Westminster Press, 1960), p. 400. McNeill helpfully indicated the dates when the various parts of the *Institutes* were composed but he failed to note the significance of the dates in connection with the fourth commandment.

[12] *Sermons on Genesis,* Chapters 1-11, trans. Rob Roy McGregor (Edinburgh: Banner of Truth, 2009), p. 123.

come to us from the day itself which is given to us, during which we abandon all occupations, all worldly cares and thoughts in order to give our minds to that holy meditation we mentioned . . . Now in the Law, God commanded the day of rest for another reason, and at this point we must carefully distinguish between the order God established in the creation of the world and this commandment which appears in the Law of Moses . . . to give another and differing view, namely that it is a shadow and figure of spiritual rest . . . But the fact remains that we have one definite day of the week which is to be completely spent in hearing God's word, in prayers, and petitions and meditating upon his works that we may rejoice in him.

There are two facets of observance. For the present, it will suffice us to know that God continued in the Law what he had begun at the creation of the world . . . So let us learn to sanctify the day of rest in order to bring ourselves into conformity with our God's example and preserve the order which he established to be inviolable till the end.[13]

Calvin's change of judgment had already taken place by the time his *Commentary on Genesis* was published in 1554.[14] In that volume, on God's blessing of the seventh day in Genesis 2:3, he said:

That benediction is nothing else than a solemn consecration, by which God claims for himself the meditations and employments of men on the seventh day. This is, indeed,

[13] *Ibid.,* pp. 128-30.
[14] J. K. Carter, in an unpublished doctoral thesis which I have not seen, traces the change in Calvin's thought to the years 1550-59; 'Sunday Observance in Scotland 1560-1606,' Edinburgh, 1957.

the proper business of the whole of life, in which men should daily exercise themselves, to consider the infinite goodness, justice, power, and wisdom of God, in this magnificent theatre of heaven and earth. But, lest men should prove less sedulously attentive to it than they ought, every seventh day has been especially selected for the purpose of supplying what was wanting in daily meditation . . . he dedicated every seventh day to rest, that his own example might be a perpetual rule.[15]

THE NEW TESTAMENT
AND THE COMMANDMENT

We are not yet done with the case that the New Testament has terminated the fourth commandment. Two arguments are advanced to support that case.

1. The Apostle Paul, it is said, speaks against treating particular days as special. He remonstrates with professing Christians for observing 'days and months and seasons and years' (*Gal.* 4:10). Regard for particular days he identifies with 'one who is weak in faith' (*Rom.* 14:1). In Colossians 2:16-17, 'a festival or a new moon, or a Sabbath day' are referred to as 'a mere shadow of what

---

[15] *Commentary on Genesis* (Calvin Trans. Soc.; repr. Edinburgh: Banner of Truth, 1965), pp. 105-6. That the Genesis 2:2-3 pattern remains for us to follow today is again asserted in the reformer's final commentary (1563), *Commentaries of the Four Last Books of Moses,* vol. 2 (Calvin Trans. Soc.), p. 437. There are variations of emphasis in Calvin's thought which cannot be explored here. See *Institutes of the Christian Religion,* pp. 394-400. Also, Fairbairn, *Typology of Scripture* pp. 140-42, 513-21.

is to come'. These texts, it is said, leave no room for our treating one day in seven as still blessed and sanctified by God.

In response, it may be said that there is no certainty at all that these references have to do with the keeping of the seventh day. In the ceremonial law there were other 'sabbath days', that is festivals, in addition to the weekly Sabbath.[16] But supposing the words are understood to teach a prohibition for the keeping special of any day, then a considerable inconsistency would be found in the New Testament, and in Paul's practice. For, clearly, there was just such a day observed in apostolic practice. Consider the evidence:

• The raising of financial aid for the needy was integral to the life of the churches, and Paul tells the church at Corinth, that the putting aside of aid for others was to be a duty on 'the first day of every week'. But this statement is introduced by words which

---

[16] 'Nor must it be forgotten that the Sabbath was under the Old Testament an integral part of a cycle of feasts which is no longer in force now. The type embodied in it was deepened by the Sabbatical Year and the Year of Jubilee. On the Sabbath man and beast rested, in the Sabbatical Year the very soil rests … From all this we have been released by the work of Christ, but not from the Sabbath as instituted at Creation.' Vos, *Biblical Theology,* pp. 142-3. 'The Colossian Christian who declined the ceremonial observance of the Sabbath in this respect was right. An altogether different question arises when the Christian is asked to "secularize" the weekly Rest which descends to us from the days of Paradise, and which is as vitally necessary as ever for man's physical and spiritual well-being.' H.C.G.Moule, *Colossians and Philemon* (Cambridge: University Press, 1893), p. 110. On the words of Romans 14:5 ('One man esteems one day above another'), John Murray writes that to treat this as a reference to the Lord's day and the weekly sabbath, 'brings us into conflict with principles that are embedded in the total witness of Scripture.' It supposes that 'the beneficent design contemplated in the original institution (*Mark* 2:28) has no application under the gospel, and the lordship Christ exercised over the Sabbath was for the purpose of abolishing it.' John Murray, *Epistle to the Romans,* vol. 2 (Grand Rapids: Eerdmans, 1965), p. 259.

show the direction was not one for observation at Corinth alone: 'Now concerning the collection for the saints, as I directed the churches of Galatia, so do you also. On the first day of every week let each one of you put aside and save . . .' (*1 Cor.* 16:1-2).

• Acts 20:7 says something more on the practice of Christians on the first day of the week. When taking ship towards Syria, Paul stopped at Troas and stayed, writes Luke, seven days; it would be natural to believe that the reason for his staying lies in the words that follow: 'And on the first day of the week, when we were gathered together to break bread, Paul began talking to them, intending to depart the next day, and he prolonged his message until midnight.' The 'first day' has all the appearance of a stated meeting of Christians.

• Another apostle, the beloved John, writing by the Holy Spirit's guidance, adds information which is very significant. In an almost incidental reference, he indicates that the first day of the week was honoured by Christians with the highest of titles. A new name had entered history. On Patmos he writes: 'I was in the Spirit on the Lord's day' (*Rev.* 1:10). How can we be sure that in these words John was speaking of the first day of the week? Because of the testimony that exists from the earliest years of the post-apostolic age. The day which the Roman world called 'Sunday' was known to Christians as 'the Lord's day'. Ignatius, a younger contemporary of John's, who died about the year A.D. 107, spoke of Christians as 'no longer observing Sabbaths, but fashioning our lives according to the Lord's day, on which our life arose through him'.[17] For Christians the special day had become

[17] Irenaeus, Tertullian, Clement of Alexandria, Origen and Cyprian, all speak of the first day of the week as 'the Lord's day'. Tertullian said: 'We celebrate the

the first day of the week. In the words of Philip Schaff, one of the most dependable of historians, 'The universal and uncontradicted Sunday observance in the second century can only be explained by the fact that it had its roots in apostolic practice.'[18]

J. C. Ryle comments: 'Why we are told so pointedly about the "first day of the week" and the "Lord's day", if the Apostles kept no one day more holy than another, is to my mind inexplicable.'[19]

But if we accept this information, what does it have to do with believing that the Lord's day has any connexion with the fourth commandment? The key question is this: if there was a transference of spiritual significance from the seventh day to the first, who authorised the change? To think the New Testament provides no light on that question is surely a mistake. The special day appointed by God in the Old Testament was surrounded

---

day after Saturday in distinction from those who call this day their Sabbath . . . All anxiety to be abstained from, and business postponed on the Lord's Day.' Eusebius wrote: 'All things that it was duty to do on the Sabbath, these have we transferred to the Lord's day, as more appropriately belong to it, because it has a precedence and is first in rank, and more honourable than the Jewish Sabbath. For in that day, in making the world, God said, Let there be light, and there was light; and on the same day the Sun of righteousness arose upon our souls.' When the early Christians were asked, 'Have you kept the Lord's day?' (*Servasti Dominicum?*), they replied, 'I am a Christian, I cannot but keep it' (*Christianus sum, omittere non possum*). For a fuller record of early church evidence see, 'The Literature of the Sabbath Question', (*British and Foreign Evangelical Review*, vol. 15, pp. 570-96, and R. T. Beckwith and W. Stott, *The Christian Sunday: A Biblical and Historical Study* (Grand Rapids; Baker, 1980).

[18] Schaff, *History of the Christian Church: Apostolic Christianity*, vol. 2 (Edinburgh: Clark, 1893), pp. 479. He adds: Such observance is the more to be appreciated as it had no support in civil legislation before the age of Constantine, and must have been connected with many inconveniences, considering the lowly social condition of the majority of Christians and their dependence on their heathen masters and employers.'

[19] Ryle, *Knots Untied*, p. 366.

by his authority. It was found in the first table of the law. It was not open for any man-made additions or alterations. God called it 'My holy day'. He alone regulated its use, and guarded it by solemn sanctions. Therefore when Jesus said, 'the Son of Man is Lord even of the Sabbath', he was claiming the prerogative of deity (*Mark* 2:28). Later, after asserting his possession of 'all authority in heaven and on earth', the Lord placed an all-important limitation on the authority of the apostles and the church with the words, 'teaching them to observe all that I have commanded you' (*Matt.* 28:20).

In the light of such words it is unthinkable that men changed the seventh day to the first without the authority of the one to whom that day belongs. That Christ's authority was behind the transference is surely implicit in the language of the apostle John. In speaking of 'the Lord's day' he uses the very same language as is used of 'the Lord's Supper' (*1 Cor.* 11:20). 'The Lord's Supper' means the supper that Christ appointed and over which he presides. The first day of the week could never have been described as 'the Lord's' if Jesus had not himself commanded it.

I conclude, then, that the warnings of Paul against the superstitious use of days, and against the retention of national and ceremonial restrictions belonging to the Sabbath in the Mosaic economy, in no way invalidates the principle of one day in seven kept specially for God, as taught in the fourth commandment, and beginning with the Genesis pattern.

2. A second and last argument remains. In brief it is that the Old Testament commandment on the seventh day foreshadowed the 'rest' that was to come in Christ; therefore, for believers who have 'entered into rest', the meaning is now fulfilled, and to go back to the commandment would be to go back to 'law'.

Some would add, 'you are not under law but under grace' (*Rom.* 6:14).[20]

There is an important element of truth here. When rest in God was lost by man at the Fall, the divine purpose for the restoration of that rest lay in the future work of Christ. No man would come to that rest except he first come to faith in the promised Saviour. The fourth chapter of the Epistle to the Hebrews speaks of three 'rests': the rest of creation, when God rested from his works; the rest typified by the entering of Canaan; and the rest now obtained by Christ 'for the people of God'. 'For the one [*i.e.* Christ] who has entered His rest has himself also rested from his works, as God did from His' (*Heb.* 4:10).[21] As creation first gave delight and rest to God, the finished work of Christ is a yet more glorious rest. In that work Christ is 'satisfied' (*Isa.* 53:11), and in his 'beloved Son' the Father is 'well-pleased' (*Matt.* 17:5). United to Christ and righteous in him, we are redeemed for the glory of God, and see that glory 'in the face of Christ' (*2 Cor.* 4:6). Here is something greater than the first creation. In the church God says, 'This is My resting place forever; here I will dwell, for I have desired it' (*Psa.* 132:14).

[20] This text is often misunderstood. To be 'under law' is descriptive of all men by nature, it is to be under wrath. But Christ's fulfilment of the demands and penalties of the law places all who belong to him in an entirely new position. Their obligation to law has been met in Christ, and having received new life in him, sin no longer has the mastery over them. This is what Paul means by 'not under law'. Yet there is no contradiction when, at the same time, he asserts that in the gospel message, 'we establish the law' (*Rom.* 3:31, AV), indeed, that is the very purpose of the gospel (*Rom.* 8:4).

[21] This understanding of 'one who has entered his rest' is considered by many commentators to be speaking of the action of the believer; but if that were the case 'as God did from his' ceases to be of parallel, for the believer ceases from *sinful* works. See Owen, *Hebrews,* vol. 4, pp. 332-4. Some hold that the fourth commandment included a type, intended to teach Israel to cease from their own sinful works. I know no evidence for this opinion, save that all law in its Mosaic form brought home man's bondage to sin (*Gal.* 3:19-24).

All this is wonderfully true, but why should the fulfilment of redemption make impossible the observance of a special day? Is it not rather entirely in harmony with revelation to believe that the first day of the week — the day when the early Christians greeted one another with 'Christ is risen!' — takes and continues what is in the fourth commandment and Genesis 2:3? Could any day be more suitable for special commemoration? Redemption has been accomplished: 'The stone which the builders rejected has become the chief corner stone. This is the Lord's doing; it is marvelous in our eyes. This is the day which the Lord has made; let us rejoice and be glad in it' (*Psa.* 118:22-24; *Matt.* 21:42; *Acts* 4:11).

It is granted that a dispensation of law under Moses was in preparation for Christ. Granted, too, that the gospel is a presentation of grace; but to go back to the practice of the substance of the fourth commandment — indeed to any of the ten commandments — is not to go to law as a means of justification, no more than the original pattern of Genesis 2:3 was in order to justification. The great difference for the Christian now is not that the law is no rule for him, it is that he has received a power and motive to obey that he never had before.

The Christian loves the law of God — 'joyfully concurs' with it (*Rom.* 7:22) — not in order to gain acceptance with God, but because his nature is being restored to likeness with God. This was the great Old Testament promise of the New Covenant: 'For this is the covenant that I will make with the house of Israel after those days, says the Lord: I will put My laws into their minds, and I will write them upon their hearts. And I will be their God, and they shall be My people' (*Heb.* 8:10).[22] Or, stated in the clear

---

[22] 'The law sends us to the gospel for our justification; the gospel sends us to the law to frame our way of life . . . We cry down works in opposition to grace

language of fulfilment: 'For what the Law could not do, weak as it was through the flesh, God did: sending His own Son in the likeness of sinful flesh and as an offering for sin, He condemned sin in the flesh, in order that the requirement of the Law might be fulfilled in us, who do not walk according to the flesh, but according to the Spirit' (*Rom.* 8:3-4).

Christians have been set free to obey the law as 'the law of liberty'. They can say with William Cowper,

> *To see the law by Christ fulfilled*
> *And hear His pardoning voice*
> *Changes the slave into a child*
> *And duty into choice.*[23]

Of the fourth commandment Christ's words are therefore true, 'Do not think that I came to abolish the Law or the Prophets; I did not come to abolish, but to fulfill' (*Matt.* 5:17). The Pharisees had made the Sabbath a day of religious drudgery, of narrow external duties, all supposedly meritorious. This was what Christ rejected, but as Ryle says, he 'no more abolishes the Sabbath, than a man destroys a house when he cleans the moss or weeds off the roof'.[24]

It is a serious misunderstanding of the New Testament to regard a careful obedience to the law of God as 'legalism'. On the contrary, it is proof of a true relationship with the Saviour.

---

in justification, and we cry up obedience as the fruits of grace in sanctification.' Samuel Bolton, *The True Bounds of Christian Freedom* (Edinburgh: Banner of Truth, repr. 2001), pp.11, 68-9.

[23] From the hymn, 'No strength of nature can suffice.'

[24] J. C. Ryle, *Knots Untied*, p. 365. 'So little does Jesus imagine that the Ten Commandments were of local and temporary obligation that he treats them as the law of the universal and eternal kingdom which he came to establish.' B. B. Warfield, *Shorter Writings* (Nutley, NJ: Presbyterian and Reformed, 1970), vol. 1, p. 313.

'The one who says, "I have come to know Him," and does not keep His commandments, is a liar, and the truth is not in him' (*1 John* 2:4).

'Why should insistence on Sabbath observance be pharisaical or legalistic? The question is: Is it a divine ordinance? If it is, then adherence to it is not legalistic any more than adherence to the other commandments of God. Are we to be charged with legalism because we are meticulously honest? If we are jealous not to deprive our neighbour of one penny which is his, and are therefore meticulous in the details of money transactions, are we necessarily legalistic? Our Christianity is not worth much if we can knowingly and deliberately deprive our neighbour of one penny that belongs to him and not to us. Are we to be charged with legalism if we are scrupulously chaste and condemn the very suggestion or gesture of lewdness? How distorted our conception of the Christian ethic and of the demands of holiness has become if we associate concern for details of integrity with pharisaism and legalism! 'He that is faithful in that which is least is faithful also in much: and he that is unjust in the least is unjust also in much' (*Luke* 16:10, AV).'[25]

THE WITNESS OF HISTORY

Christians do not appeal to post-biblical history and tradition as authoritative revelation of the will of God. Nonetheless, if the question is asked whether there is evidence from history that God has continued to give special blessing through one day in

[25] John Murray, *Collected Writings,* vol 1, (Edinburgh: Banner of Truth, 1976), pp. 214-5.

seven, I believe there is. Repeatedly in periods when the Holy Spirit has revived the church, and when the Scriptures have been addressed with new seriousness, the fourth commandment has been recovered and there has been new health in the churches. While there was Sunday observance of a kind when the Reformation of the sixteenth century began, it was only when the power of the gospel was known that the spiritual keeping of the day was restored. Martin Luther preached,

> The Sabbath day is undoubtedly rooted in nature; in our human nature and in the nature of the created universe . . . It is Jehovah who made the Sabbath; though for man, the Sabbath is not of man, but has come to man as a gift of God himself.[26]

In the Puritan period which followed the Reformation in England, the life and power of Christianity was closely identified with the conviction that a seventh day blessing continues in Christ's appointment of the first day. Thus Thomas Brooks can write:

> Remember this, that there are no Christians in all the world comparable to those, for the power of godliness and the heights of grace, holiness, and communion with God, who are most strict, serious, studious and conscientious in sanctifying of the Lord's day.[27]

Likewise John Owen in 1671:

> If I have ever seen anything in the ways and worship of God wherein the power of religion or godliness hath been expressed

[26] *Lectures on Genesis, Luther's Works,* ed. Jaroslav Pelikan (Saint Louis, Concordia, 1958), vol. 1, p. 80.

[27] *Works of Thomas Brooks,* vol. 6 (Edinburgh: Banner of Truth), pp. 305-6.

. . . it hath been there and with them where and amongst whom the Lord's day hath been had in highest esteem.[28]

The history of evangelical awakenings shows that an outpouring of the Spirit has brought a new desire to keep the Lord's day holy. So it was in Wales, in the Highlands of Scotland, and in many of the mission fields of the world, in the eighteenth and nineteenth centuries. One period of awakening in Wales began as John Elias preached one Sunday at Rhuddlan. It was the normal day for fairs and markets, and the place was crowded with those who had no thought of the fourth commandment. Friends had warned Elias that there was danger in what he proposed to do, but he went ahead, and on the steps of the New Inn preached on the words of Exodus 34:21, 'You shall work six days, but on the seventh day you shall rest; even during plowing time and harvest you shall rest.'[29] The authority of God was so upon the word preached that the use of the Lord's day in that area was changed for generations to come.

The honouring of the fourth commandment has brought blessings to nations. Dr J. H. Merle d'Aubigné, visiting Britain in 1845, included these words in his description of the country:

> One of the features which most completely brings out the character of British Christianity, is the observance of the Lord's day, or the Sabbath as they term it, I think, improperly . . . I do not hesitate to say, that this submission of a whole people to the law of God, is very impressive and is

[28] Owen, *Hebrews,* vol. 2, pp. 428-9.

[29] This remarkable occasion and its results is fully described in Edward Morgan, *John Elias: Life, Letters and Essays* (repr. Edinburgh: Banner of Truth, 1973), pp. 86-89. See also pp. 397-99. Modern translations correctly render 'earing' as 'ploughing'; not that the Authorised Version is wrong, for ploughing is the meaning of the Saxon word 'erian' as the AV translators knew.

probably the most incontestable source of the many blessings that have been showered on the nation. Order and obedience, morality and power, are all in Britain connected with the observation of the Sunday.[30]

On the other side of the Atlantic, Philip Schaff wrote of the Sabbath:

The due observance of it, in which the churches of England, Scotland and America, to their incalculable advantage, excel the churches of the European continent, is a wholesome school of discipline, a means of grace for the people, a safeguard of public morality and religion, a bulwark against infidelity, and a source of immeasurable blessing to the church, the state, and family. Next to the church and the Bible, the Lord's Day is the chief pillar of Christian society.[31]

It is true where 'keeping Sunday' has not been accompanied by a right understanding of the meaning of the day, the observance has become a dead formality. But among those whose intention is the honouring of God in the keeping of the day, the liveliest and happiest form of Christianity has commonly been found. This was once so evident that Robert Murray M'Cheyne could ask the question: 'Did you ever meet with a lively believer in

[30] J. H. Merle d'Aubigné, *Germany, England, and Scotland, or Recollections of a Swiss Minister* (London: Simpkin, Marshall, 1848), pp. 105, 108-9.
[31] Schaff, *Apostolic Christianity*, p. 479. For the same conviction in J. C. Ryle, see *Knots Untied*, pp. 371-2. This belief was not confined to evangelical Christians. Lord Macaulay, speaking on the 'Ten Hours Bill' in Parliament, said, 'We are not poorer but richer, because we have, through many ages, rested from our labour one day in seven.' Prime Minister W. E. Gladstone believed: 'The religious observance of Sunday is a main prop of the religious character of the country. From a moral, social, and physical point of view, the observance of Sunday is a duty of absolute consequence.'

any country under heaven — one who loved Christ, and lived a holy life — who did not delight in keeping holy to God the entire Lord's day?'[32]

On this subject our Lord's words surely remain relevant: 'You will know them by their fruits' (*Matt.* 7:16).

CONCLUSIONS

1. To quote Schaff once more:

In the gospel dispensation the Sabbath is not a degradation, but an elevation of the week to a higher plane, looking to the consecration of all time and work. It is not a legal ceremonial bondage, but rather a precious gift of grace, a privilege, a holy rest in God in the midst of the unrest of the world, a day of spiritual refreshing in communion with God and in the fellowship of the saints, a foretaste and pledge of the never-ending Sabbath in heaven.[33]

2. Understanding the observation of the first day of the week as the day of Christ's resurrection points to the evangelistic imperative. No one but a Christian can begin a right keeping of the Lord's day. A spiritual day requires a spiritual life. As John Newton once wrote, 'How dull the Sabbath day, without the Sabbath's Lord'. There can be no delight in Christ's day until his resurrection and redeeming love are known. Only in the rebirth of

---

[32] *Memoir and Remains of R. M. M'Cheyne,* ed. A. Bonar (repr. Edinburgh: Banner of Truth, 2009), p. 601. Many in Scotland said this before M'Cheyne. For instance, John Willison (1680-1750): 'Wherever religion flourishes in the power of it, there it is that most conscience is made in the observation of the Sabbath.' *Practical Works of John Willison* (Edinburgh: Blackie, 1844), p. 111.

[33] Schaff, *Apostolic Christianity,* p. 479.

a sinner does a recovery of the rest in the God of paradise begin. For this person, as Philip Henry once said, the command is 'an easy, sweet command'.[34] Those who come to Jesus for 'rest' sing with Charles Wesley,

> *Jesus, Thou art all I want,*
> *More than all in Thee I find.*

It was no great sacrifice for Eric Liddell in 1924 to pass by the opportunity for a gold medal in the 100 metres in the Paris Olympics rather than to run on the Lord's day. He was already enjoying something far greater.

A true understanding of the Lord's day must lead to compassion for non-Christians and a deeper concern to make Christ known. Ignorance of the fourth commandment is often an obstacle to salvation. 'I had no Sundays', was the admission of a dying London taxi driver, unprepared to leave the world.

If the creation of the material universe should be kept in perpetual remembrance, how much more the new creation secured by the resurrection of Jesus Christ from the dead. If men wish the knowledge of that event to die out, let them neglect to keep holy the first day of the week; if they desire that event to be everywhere known and remembered, let them consecrate that day to the worship of the risen Saviour. This is God's method for keeping the resurrection of Christ, on which our salvation depends, in perpetual remembrance.

God has given the world the Church, the Bible, the ministry, the sacraments; these are not human devices. And can it be supposed that the Sabbath, without which

[34] *The Lives of Philip and Matthew Henry,* J. B. Williams (repr. Edinburgh: Banner of Truth, 1974), vol. 1. p. 373.

all these divine institutions would be immeasurably inefficient, should be left to the will or wisdom of men? This is not to be supposed. That these divinely appointed means for the illumination and sanctification of men, are in great measure without effect, where the Sabbath is neglected or profaned, is a matter of experience.[35]

3. The inability of the non-Christian to keep the Lord's day in no way lessens their responsibility to keep it. The obligation rests upon the eternal principles set out in the moral law. Fallen man can, of himself, keep none of the ten commandments truly, yet he is still held to account for the obedience which God requires. Man's hostility to the fourth commandment is part of the antagonism with which he reacts to God himself (*Rom.* 8:7). Teaching the law of God, as Christ taught it, is a vital part of the witness of the church, for 'by the law is the knowledge of sin' (*Rom.* 3:20; 7:7, AV), for without that knowledge there is no repentance, and without repentance no salvation. Antinomianism, which discounts the ten commandments, is therefore contrary to biblical evangelism.

4. The moral law of God exists for mankind. Accordingly the Protestant nations professing Christianity buttressed the observation of the first day of the week with civil penalties. It was understood that reverence for God was necessary for the well being of a people and that it included respect for the day God has appointed. People have now largely forgotten how far this principle was once embedded in national life. In the nineteenth century Charles Hodge could write in the United States:

---

[36] George W. Bethune, *Guilt, Grace and Gratitude* (repr. Edinburgh: Banner of Truth, 2001), vol 2, p. 487.

Christianity forbids all unnecessary labour, or the transaction of worldly business, on the Lord's Day . . . All public offices are closed, and all official business is suspended. From Maine to Georgia, from ocean to ocean, one day in the week, by the law of God and by the law of the land, the people rest.[36]

It is the argument of atheists that the state should have nothing to do with personal behaviour. Marriage law (until recently upheld by 'Christian' countries) stands on the same basis in Genesis 2 as does the seven-day cycle. Both should be upheld by governments. That contempt for God and the ten commandments brings judgments on nations is a clear truth in Scripture. And the most common form of such judgment is the removal of spiritual blessings (2 *Chron.* 36:17-21; *Jer.* 17:27; *Lam.* 2:6; *Ezek.* 22 :26-31). An observation that William Hewitson once made in Germany has universal application: 'Germany tells me, that if Scotland lose her Sabbaths, she will lose along with them her religion and her God.'[37]

Some believe that for Christians to bear witness to the fourth commandment in an unsympathetic world would be to impede evangelism. The reverse has tragically proved to be true. Bishop Ryle understood what would happen in England if Sunday became as any other day:

Break down the fence which now surrounds the Sunday, and our Sunday schools will soon come to an end. Let in the flood of worldliness and pleasure-seeking on the Lord's day, without check or hindrance, and our congregations will soon dwindle away. There is not too much religion in the

[36] Charles Hodge, *Systematic Theology,* vol. 3, p. 344.
[37] *Memoir of W. H. Hewitson,* John Baillie (London: Nisbet, 1874), p. 72.

land now. Destroy the sanctity of the Sabbath, and there will soon be far less . . . It would be a joy to the infidel; but it would be an insult and offence to God.[38]

It is true that civil law can only restrain public disregard for the Lord's day, but to argue against the limited use of law to no use at all has been proved folly.

5. As already said, there ought to be no problem for Christians about how to observe the Lord's day. They will seek to 'remember' it before it comes, so that nothing is postponed to that day that can be done before. They will remember it is still a 'day' God has set apart from the ordinary engagements of life, and not part of a day.[39] Apart from works of 'necessity and mercy' the desire will be to arrange the day so that there is a maximum of time free from distractions of the affairs of the week. The faithful support of public worship ought to be beyond question, along with private time for spiritual things, especially for reading, meditation, and prayer. Christ is risen and he gives the Holy Spirit to us, as well as to the apostle John on Patmos.

But as Christians know, there are complications in the right keeping of the day. The first responsibility belongs to heads of

---

[38] *Knots Untied,* p. 361. Ryle knew very well that Sunday laws make no one Christian, but they did something to keep the day special and to encourage church going. Many were brought to hear the Bible, and public respect for God spread through national life to a degree scarcely conceivable today.

[39] Sir Walter Scott observed, 'Give to the world one half of Sunday and you will find that religion has no strong hold on the other.' 'Not a part, but the whole day is the Lord's; and it is as dangerous to halve it with God in point of time, as it was for Ananias and Sapphira to halve their dedicated goods, and bring in but a part.' John Flavel, on the fourth commandment, *Works* (repr. London; Banner of Truth, 1968), vol. 6, p. 234. R. L. Dabney closed a last letter to his children before his death with the words, 'Remember the Sabbath day to keep it holy.' *Life and Letters of Robert Lewis Dabney,* T. C. Johnson (Edinburgh; Banner of Truth, 1977), p. 523.

households (*Exod.* 20:10), and where that is neglected, believers may find — as Christian slaves in the first century — that in such households time is not freely their own. And what do believing parents do with children and young people in their families who, as yet, have no heart for spiritual things? The answer has to be along the lines of making the day as bright and happy for them as possible, while not neglecting the obedience God requires. Many who became Christians in later years have looked back on their Sundays in a serious Christian home as a great and formulating privilege. By parental example, as well as word, they were taught,

> *A Sabbath well spent*
> *Brings a week of content*
> *And strength for the toils of the morrow;*
> *But a Sabbath profaned,*
> *Whate'er may be gained*
> *Is a certain forerunner of sorrow.*

For young and old, the rest on earth prepares for the rest in heaven.

'There cannot be a more lively resemblance on this side heaven than the sanctifying of the Sabbath in a heavenly manner.'[40]

'There can be, after the gospel, no blessing so high as that of the Sabbath, no privilege so great as that which it affords, no dignity so noble as that to which it introduces us.'[41]

[40] Thomas Brooks, *Works,* vol. 6, p. 112.
[41] B. B. Warfield, *Shorter Writings* (Nutley, NJ: Presbyterian and Reformed, 1970) vol. 1, p. 309.

SOME OTHER BOOKS
ON THIS SUBJECT
PUBLISHED BY THE TRUST

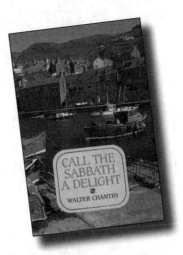

Call the Sabbath a Delight
Walter J Chantry

Walter Chantry is an author who has consistently put his finger on the particular weaknesses and failures of the contemporary church. In his books we hear echoes of the prophetic insights and warnings which run through Scripture. *Call the Sabbath a Delight* is no exception. Its title indicates the burden of its message. A startling transformation has taken place in the way Christians approach the Lord's Day. While Walter Chantry does not flinch from stressing that the effects of this have been disastrous—morally and socially, as well as spiritually—his burden is not morally negative. His concern is to show why and how the Lord's Day is meant to be one of joy and blessing for God's people. He succeeds in a remarkable way. *Call the Sabbath a Delight* is written with a deep pastoral concern. It is an important book for all Christians to read.

112 pages, paperback
ISBN 978 0 85151 588 5

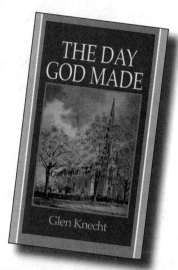

The Day God Made
Glen C. Knecht

Do Christians today see the Lord's Day, the Christian Sabbath, as an unattractive, dreary time of legalistic restriction? If so, have they misunderstood the nature of 'the day God made'? Glen Knecht believes that many have. They have taken what was meant to be 'a little oasis of greenness, for meditation and rest', to be an arid period of irksome inactivity, and have rejected a good gift of God which should have been welcomed and used with joy. Knecht sees the day as rooted in Creation and the teaching and example of Christ, as well as in the Ten Commandments. He urges a return to the right use of this 'little section of time fenced off by God for the restoration and blessing of His people' as a time in which to meditate, rest, serve others, and grow in understanding of God's ways and love.

112 pages, paperback
ISBN 978 0 85151 851 0

OTHER BOOKLETS BY IAIN H. MURRAY
PUBLISHED BY THE TRUST

The Cross, the Pulpit of God's Love
The Invitation System
The Psalter—the Only Hymnal?
The Unresolved Controversy

For details of other helpful publications please contact

THE BANNER OF TRUTH TRUST

3 Murrayfield Road,   P O Box 621, Carlisle,
Edinburgh EH12 6EL   Pennsylvania 17013,
           UK   USA

www.banneroftruth.co.uk